D0787881

PRESIDENTS

RONALD REAGAN

A MyReportLinks.com Book

Donald Henry Hinkle

 MyReportLinks.com Books
an imprint of
Enslow Publishers, Inc.
Box 398, 40 Industrial Road
Berkeley Heights, NJ 07922
USA

MyReportLinks.com Books, an imprint of Enslow Publishers, Inc. MyReportLinks is a trademark of Enslow Publishers, Inc.

Library of Congress Cataloging-in-Publication Data

Hinkle, Donald (Donald Henry)
  Ronald Reagan / Donald Hinkle.
     p. cm. — (Presidents)
Summary: A biography of the fortieth president of the United States.
Includes bibliographical references and index.
  ISBN 0-7660-5112-9
  1. Reagan, Ronald—Juvenile literature. 2. Presidents—United
States—Biography—Juvenile literature. [1. Reagan, Ronald. 2.
Presidents.] I. Title. II. Series.
  E877 .H56 2002
  973.927'092—dc21
                            2002014116

To Our Readers:
Through the purchase of this book, you and your library gain access to the Report Links that specifically back up this book.

The Publisher will provide access to the Report Links that back up this book and will keep these Report Links up to date on **www.myreportlinks.com** for three years from the book's first publication date.

We have done our best to make sure all Internet addresses in this book were active and appropriate when we went to press. However, the author and the Publisher have no control over, and assume no liability for, the material available on those Internet sites or on other Web sites they may link to.

The usage of the MyReportLinks.com Books Web site is subject to the terms and conditions stated on the Usage Policy Statement on **www.myreportlinks.com**.

In the future, a password may be required to access the Report Links that back up this book. The password is found on the bottom of page 4 of this book.

Any comments or suggestions can be sent by e-mail to comments@myreportlinks.com or to the address on the back cover.

Photo Credits: © Corel Corporation, pp. 1 (background), 3; MyReportLinks.com Books, p. 4; PBS, *The American Experience*, pp. 19, 23, 37; Ronald Reagan Presidential Library, pp. 1, 11, 14, 16, 18, 25, 26, 31, 33, 35, 39, 41, 43; The American President, p. 29; The Brady Center to Prevent Gun Violence, p. 13; The Reagan Foundation, p. 21.

Cover Photo: © Corel Corporation; Ronald Reagan Presidential Library.

Contents

MyReportLinks.com Books
Great Books, Great Links, Great for Research!

MyReportLinks.com Books present the information you need to learn about your report subject. In addition, they show you where to go on the Internet for more information. The pre-evaluated Report Links that back up this book are kept up to date on **www.myreportlinks.com**. With the purchase of a MyReportLinks.com Books title, you and your library gain access to the Report Links that specifically back up that book. The Report Links save hours of research time and link to dozens—even hundreds—of Web sites, source documents, and photos related to your report topic.

Please see "To Our Readers" on the Copyright page for important information about this book, the MyReportLinks.com Books Web site, and the Report Links that back up this book.

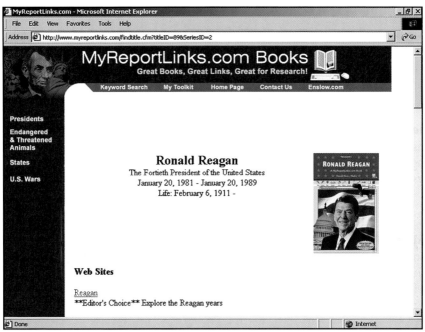

Access:

The Publisher will provide access to the Report Links that back up this book and will try to keep these Report Links up to date on our Web site for three years from the book's first publication date. Please enter **PRE4395** if asked for a password.

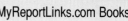

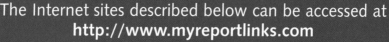

The Internet sites described below can be accessed at
http://www.myreportlinks.com

*EDITOR'S CHOICE

▶ **Reagan**
At this PBS Web site you can explore the Reagan years by taking a
virtual tour through the Reagan Presidential Library. You can also read
quotations and excerpts from two of his biographies and view a time
line of important events in his life.

Link to this Internet site from http://www.myreportlinks.com
*EDITOR'S CHOICE

▶ **Ronald Reagan Presidential Library**
The Ronald Reagan Presidential Library holds biographical sketches of
Ronald and Nancy Reagan, the text of President Reagan's speeches, and
a collection of photographs of the Reagans.

Link to this Internet site from http://www.myreportlinks.com
*EDITOR'S CHOICE

▶ **The "Prime-Time" President**
The American President Web site provides "Fast Facts" about Reagan
and a brief introduction to his administrations. You will also find a
detailed description of his life before his presidency as well as his legacy.

Link to this Internet site from http://www.myreportlinks.com
*EDITOR'S CHOICE

▶ **The Trial of John Hinckley**
This Web site explores John Hinckley's attempt to assassinate Ronald
Reagan and Hinckley's obsession with Jody Foster and the film *Taxi
Driver*. You will also find trial testimony and photographs.

Link to this Internet site from http://www.myreportlinks.com
*EDITOR'S CHOICE

▶ **Objects From the Presidency**
By navigating through this site you will find objects related to all of the
United States presidents, including Ronald Reagan. You can also read a
brief description of the era he lives in and learn about the office of
the presidency.

Link to this Internet site from http://www.myreportlinks.com
*EDITOR'S CHOICE

▶ **The Fifteenth Anniversary of "Star Wars":
Big Budgets but Little Progress**
This Web site explores the progress of the Strategic Defense Initiative, or
"Star Wars," Reagan's plan of defense against nuclear-armed ballistic missiles.
Here you will learn why this project has never been completed.

Link to this Internet site from http://www.myreportlinks.com

The Internet sites described below can be accessed at
http://www.myreportlinks.com

▶**The American Presidency: Iran-Contra Affair**
The American Presidency Web site provides a brief overview of the foreign
policy scandal of the Reagan administration known as the Iran-contra affair.

Link to this Internet site from http://www.myreportlinks.com

▶**The American Presidency: Ronald Reagan**
The American Presidency Web site provides an overview of Ronald Reagan's
early life and presidency. Here you will learn about his presidential campaigns,
domestic and foreign policy, and his legacy.

Link to this Internet site from http://www.myreportlinks.com

▶**American Presidents: Life Portraits: Ronald Reagan**
The American President Web site provides "Life Facts" and "Did you know?"
trivia about Ronald Reagan. You will also find a letter written by Ronald
Reagan to the American public about his illness, Alzheimer's disease.

Link to this Internet site from http://www.myreportlinks.com

▶**Brady Center to Prevent Gun Violence**
In 1981, James Brady, press secretary to President Ronald Reagan, was shot
during the assassination attempt on the president. This Web site explores the
efforts of James and Sarah Brady to stop gun violence.

Link to this Internet site from http://www.myreportlinks.com

▶**Character Above All: Ronald Reagan**
At this Web site you will find an excerpt from an essay by Peggy Noonan
about Ronald Reagan's character. Noonan was a speechwriter for Presidents
Reagan and Bush.

Link to this Internet site from http://www.myreportlinks.com

▶**Cold War**
CNN provides a comprehensive look at the Cold War, with articles
about Cold War technology, espionage, and the bomb. By clicking on
"Episode-by-Episode" you will learn about Reagan and the Star Wars
antimissile system program.

Link to this Internet site from http://www.myreportlinks.com

Report Links

The Internet sites described below can be accessed at
http://www.myreportlinks.com

▶**The Cold War: The 80s**
At this Web site you will learn about the Cold War during the 1980s.
Some events covered are the 1980 Olympics, the invasion of Grenada,
and Star Wars.

Link to this Internet site from http://www.myreportlinks.com

▶**Debating Our Destiny**
At this Web site you can read the transcripts from the 1980 presidential
debate between Ronald Reagan, Jimmy Carter, and John Anderson.
You will also find interviews with all three candidates.

Link to this Internet site from http://www.myreportlinks.com

▶**"I Do Solemnly Swear . . ."**
At this Web site you can experience Ronald Reagan's inaugurals
through images and memorabilia. You will also find the transcripts
of his inaugural addresses.

Link to this Internet site from http://www.myreportlinks.com

▶**Index to speeches by Ronald Reagan**
This Web site holds the text of three speeches made by Ronald Reagan.

Link to this Internet site from http://www.myreportlinks.com

▶**Invasion of Grenada**
In 1983, during Reagan's first administration, the United States
invaded the small Caribbean nation of Grenada. Here you will learn
about the invasion and the outcome.

Link to this Internet site from http://www.myreportlinks.com

▶**The Iran-Contra Affair: The Making of a Scandal,
1983–1988**
The Digital National Security Archives contain 4,635 documents pertaining
to the Iran-contra affair. This Web site describes the documents held in the
archive and includes photographs of the hearings.

Link to this Internet site from http://www.myreportlinks.com

Report Links

 The Internet sites described below can be accessed at
http://www.myreportlinks.com

▶**Man who shot Reagan wins mental hospital release**
This CNN article tells of a 1999 court ruling in favor of John Hinckley, who
tried to assassinate Ronald Reagan in 1981. The ruling approved supervised
visits for Hinckley away from the mental hospital he was sentenced to.

Link to this Internet site from http://www.myreportlinks.com

▶**Mr. President: Ronald Reagan**
At this Web site you will find a brief profile of Ronald Reagan, fortieth
president of the United States.

Link to this Internet site from http://www.myreportlinks.com

▶**The Presidents**
This PBS site provides profiles on many United States presidents, including
Ronald Reagan. Here you will learn about Reagan's early career, politics,
domestic policy, foreign affairs, and legacy.

Link to this Internet site from http://www.myreportlinks.com

▶**Reagan, Ronald**
The Museum of Broadcast Communications presents a brief overview of
Ronald Reagan's acting career. Reagan appeared in more than fifty movies
from 1937 to 1964.

Link to this Internet site from http://www.myreportlinks.com

▶**Ronald Reagan**
Time Magazine chose Ronald Reagan as one of its one hundred most
influential people of the twentieth century. Here you can read a four-part
article about his life and administrations.

Link to this Internet site from http://www.myreportlinks.com

▶**Ronald W. Reagan**
The World Almanac for Kids Online provides a brief overview of Ronald
Reagan. Here you will learn about his life and political career.

Link to this Internet site from http://www.myreportlinks.com

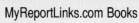
Report Links

 The Internet sites described below can be accessed at
http://www.myreportlinks.com

▶ Ronald Wilson Reagan
The Internet Public Library Web site provides facts and figures about
Ronald Reagan. Included are presidential election results, a list of
Reagan's cabinet members, notable events in his administrations,
and much more.

Link to this Internet site from http://www.myreportlinks.com

▶ Ronald Reagan: First Inaugural Address
Bartleby.com holds the text to Ronald Reagan's first inaugural address,
given on Tuesday, January 20, 1981.

Link to this Internet site from http://www.myreportlinks.com

▶ Ronald Reagan: Official Presidential Web Site
At the Ronald Reagan Foundation site you can explore the presidential
museum and archives and find speeches, quotations, and biographies. You
can also visit the "kid kabinet" to learn about other United States presidents.

Link to this Internet site from http://www.myreportlinks.com

▶ Ronald Reagan: Second Inaugural Address
Bartleby.com holds the text to Ronald Reagan's second inaugural
address, given on Monday, January 21, 1985.

Link to this Internet site from http://www.myreportlinks.com

▶ The White House: Nancy Reagan
The official White House Web site holds the biography of Nancy
Reagan. Here you will learn about her life and experiences as First Lady.

Link to this Internet site from http://www.myreportlinks.com

▶ The White House: Ronald Reagan
The official White House Web site holds the biography of Ronald
Reagan. Here you will learn about his life before the White House and
his administrations.

Link to this Internet site from http://www.myreportlinks.com

Highlights

1911—*Feb. 6:* Born in Tampico, Illinois, to Jack and Nelle Reagan.

1920—*Dec. 6:* The Reagans settle in Dixon, Illinois, the place Ronald Reagan considers his hometown.

1932—*June:* Graduates from Eureka College with a B.A. in economics and sociology.

1937—*April 20:* Is signed as a contract player for Warner Brothers Studio.

1940—*Jan. 16:* Marries Jane Wyman.

1941—*Jan. 4:* Daughter Maureen is born.

1942—*April 19:* Called to active military duty.

1945—*March 14:* Adopted son, Michael, is born.

1947—*March:* Elected president of the Screen Actors Guild for the first time.

—*Oct. 25:* Testifies before the House Un-American Activities Committee on Communism in Hollywood.

1949—*June 28:* Divorce with Wyman is finalized.

1952—*March 4:* Marries Nancy Davis.

—*Oct. 22:* Daughter Patricia is born.

1958—*May 28:* Son Ronald Prescott ("Skipper") is born.

1966—*Nov. 8:* Elected governor of California.

1970—*Nov. 3:* Reelected governor.

1980—*Nov. 4:* Elected the fortieth president of the United States, in a landslide victory.

1981—*March 30:* Survives an assassination attempt.

1984—*Nov. 6:* Wins reelection in another large victory.

1989—*Jan. 11:* Gives Farewell Address as president to the nation.

—*Jan. 20:* Leaves the White House and returns to California.

"Honey, I forgot to duck"

As an actor, Ronald Reagan had been in movies in which he was the target of fake bullets. In several movies he played a Secret Service agent named "Brass Bancroft." Two months after Ronald Reagan was inaugurated as president of the United States, a man shot him with a real bullet. And a real Secret Service agent helped save his life.

It happened after lunch on March 30, 1981. President Reagan left the White House in his bulletproof limousine (without wearing a bulletproof vest) and rode to the Washington Hilton Hotel. There, the president spoke to a

▲ This photograph of President Reagan waving farewell outside the Washington Hilton Hotel was taken just seconds before John Hinckley attempted to assassinate him on March 30, 1981.

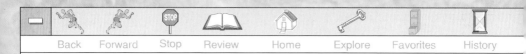
tough audience made up of hundreds of labor union leaders, who usually backed the Democrats.

The union leaders stood and applauded him even if they would have preferred a Democratic president. Reagan left the hall, surrounded by armed Secret Service agents and his press secretary, James Brady, and other aides.

▶ "Oh-oh, he's been shot"

Reporters and television cameramen waited outside. A reporter standing behind a barricade twenty feet away called to Reagan. The president smiled and waved.

And then a young blond-haired man fired five gunshots at the group. To Reagan, the shots had sounded like firecrackers. He did not realize until later that someone had been shooting at him.

As a kid, Jerry Parr had been a member of the "Brass Bancroft Junior Secret Service Club." Now, as the senior Secret Service agent at the scene, Parr shoved Reagan into the limousine and threw himself on top of the president to shield him as the car sped away.

Behind them, other agents grappled with the young man who had fired the shots. Three men lay bleeding on the sidewalk. They were James Brady and another Secret Service agent, Timothy McCarthy, and Thomas Delahanty, a Washington policeman.

The president's limousine sped toward the White House before Parr noticed blood in Reagan's mouth and realized that the president was bleeding internally. He thought that the president had suffered a broken rib when Parr threw him into the car. The car changed direction and hurtled through traffic to George Washington University Hospital. Less than four minutes later, the president walked into the hospital, though he was having trouble breathing.

Surrounded by a roomful of doctors, Reagan said, "Please tell me you're Republicans."[1] Then his legs buckled. He had lost more than half his body's blood supply and was close to death. The doctors did not know what had happened to Reagan until a nurse lifted his left arm, saw the bullet hole, and said, "Oh-oh, he's been shot."[2]

▶ Prayers and Jokes

Hearing that, Ronald Reagan mentally replayed the scene in front of the hotel and focused on the crouching figure who was shooting at him.

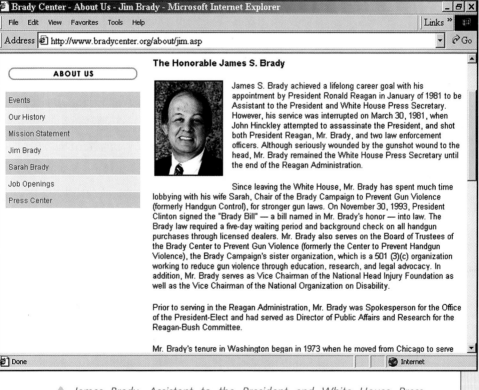

James Brady, Assistant to the President and White House Press Secretary to Ronald Reagan, suffered a gunshot wound to the head during John Hinckley's attempt to assassinate Reagan in March 1981. Despite his severe injuries, Brady remained the White House Press Secretary throughout Reagan's administrations.

He later said: ". . . I realized I couldn't ask for God's help while at the same time I felt hatred for the mixed up young man who had shot me."[3] He prayed for the young man as he had been taught to pray for others by his mother.

While doctors wheeled Reagan into the operating room, he opened his eyes and saw Nancy, his wife, bending over him. Still able to joke, he said, "Honey, I forgot to duck."[4]

Surgeons removed a .22 bullet, a "Devastator" built to explode on impact. The bullet had ricocheted off his car's armored panel, punched through Reagan's left lung, and stopped about an inch from his heart. A fit man, especially for his age, Ronald Reagan recovered rapidly. The morning

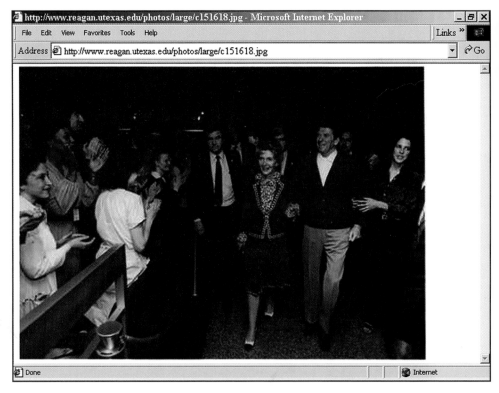

Ronald Reagan, accompanied by his wife, Nancy, and his daughter Patti, leaves George Washington University Hospital on April 11, 1981—less than two weeks after John Hinckley tried to end Reagan's life.

after he was shot, he was able to meet with some members of his staff, whom he told, jokingly, "I should have known I wasn't going to avoid a staff meeting."[5]

Recovery

The Secret Service agent and the policeman who had been shot both recovered. Reagan's press secretary had suffered more serious injuries, however. Although James Brady's head wound was first thought to be fatal, he survived. But his recovery was long, difficult, and incomplete. Later, still in a wheelchair, Brady and his wife, Sarah, endorsed a bill that limited the purchase of handguns—a bill that, before Brady's shooting, he and Ronald Reagan opposed. The bill became known as the Brady Bill.

The man who shot the president was John W. Hinckley, Jr., twenty-five years old. Hinckley had pushed into the cluster of reporters and photographers. He had looked fidgety and agitated, but nobody alerted the police or Secret Service agents. After Hinckley's arrest, the young man said that he had tried to kill the president because he believed that act would impress Jodie Foster, an actress he was infatuated with.

Ronald Reagan, the only movie star to achieve the highest office in the United States, kept his sense of humor in the face of death. As an actor, he believed that having parts in which his character died on screen was important to his career. He once said, "No actor can ask for more. Dying is the way to live in the theater."[6]

In politics, though, *almost* dying is best. His bravery and good humor further endeared Reagan to the American public. On his first night back in the White House, he wrote in his diary, "Whatever happens now I owe my life to God and will try to serve him every way I can."[7]

Chapter 2

Born "Dutch"

Nelle Wilson Reagan gave birth to a ten-pound baby during an Illinois snowstorm, on February 6, 1911. She named him Ronald Wilson Reagan.

Nelle lovingly guided his upbringing. In return, Ronald respected and admired her all her life. His father, John Edward "Jack" Reagan, and older brother, Neil, were less important in Ronald's life. His father, though, gave him a nickname at birth that would stick with him through-

out his life: Dutch.[1] The nickname had nothing to do with Ronald Reagan's ancestry. His father's family was Irish Catholic. His mother's side was Scots and English. Both parents liked to act in local plays.

▶ A Difficult Childhood

Ronald Reagan's father was a great storyteller: "No one

Young "Dutch" Reagan, third from left, in a family photo with his father, mother, and brother Neil, taken around 1914.

I ever met could tell a story better than he could," Reagan wrote.[2] His father was also an alcoholic. Ronald Reagan later referred to his father's alcoholism as "the dark demon in the bottle."[3]

Jack Reagan's addiction to alcohol was rough on the family and interfered with his earning power. "I was eleven years old," Ronald Reagan wrote in his first autobiography, "the first time I came home to find my father flat on his back on the front porch. . . . He was drunk, dead to the world. . . . I managed to drag him inside and get him to bed."[4]

Mom's Influence

Nelle Reagan was a fervent churchgoer who made Ronald attend Sunday school and every church service. Nelle also taught young Ronald to control his voice and to use it to convey thought and emotion as well as to choose words carefully.

Ronald did not do well in school, however, because he could not see clearly more than a few feet. One day, Ronald looked through his mother's glasses and learned that the world had sharp edges. "Suddenly I was able to see branches on trees and leaves on the branches."[5] He did not like wearing glasses and could not wear them while playing sports.

Dixon, Illinois

When Ronald was nine years old, the Reagans moved to Dixon, Illinois, a small town of about eight thousand people. In addition to shops, schools, and a few factories, Dixon also had a silent-movie theater and a drugstore with a soda fountain. In Dixon, Ronald got his first job, had his first taste of being a celebrity, and had his first romance.

Ronald Reagan (second row, far left, with hand on chin) and his third-grade class, 1919.

He also became interested in politics and began to focus on what he wanted to do in life.

At age fifteen, he worked as a lifeguard at the local riverside park, where a fierce undertow had caused drownings. During the seven years he lifeguarded, he carved seventy-seven notches on a log to represent the people he had saved. He enjoyed being a lifeguard: "I was the only one up there on the guard stand. It was like a stage. Everyone had to look at me."[6]

▶ First Love and High School Days

One girl who looked up at him was Margaret Cleaver, daughter of the pastor of the church that Ronald attended.

Margaret was his first and only romantic interest through high school and college. In high school, Ronald Reagan acted in school plays, wrote for the school paper, and was elected president of his senior class.

Jack Reagan was a devout Democrat. Some of his political attitudes "rubbed off" on his son Ronald, who later said, "In a small town you can't stand on the sidelines and let somebody else do what needs doing. . . . That really is how I became an activist. I felt I had to take a stand on all the controversial issues of the day; there was a sense of urgency about getting involved."[7]

The American Experience | Reagan | 3 - Microsoft Internet Explorer

File   Edit   View   Favorites   Tools   Help   Links »

Address http://www.pbs.org/wgbh/amex/reagan/gallery/03.html   Go

THE FILM & MORE
SPECIAL FEATURES
TIMELINE
GALLERY
PEOPLE & EVENTS
TEACHER'S GUIDE
AMERICAN EXPERIENCE

Reagan Family Photo album   ◀ 3 of 12 ▶

Ronald as a lifeguard, 1927

During the summers of his teenage years, Ronald Reagan worked as a lifeguard at a riverside park near Dixon. He rescued more than seventy people from drowning over those years.

College Hero

In 1928, with the money he had earned from lifeguarding, Ronald Reagan followed Margaret Cleaver to Eureka College, a small church-owned school in Illinois. Confident and cheerful, he exaggerated his football achievements in high school and won a partial football scholarship and a job on campus.

In his first year in college, Reagan got involved in a student rebellion. The country had just entered the Depression, the college was losing money, and its president wanted to cut classes and also cut back on sports. The students called a meeting and chose Ronald Reagan to voice their objections. His speech had a powerful effect: One girl fainted, and the audience voted for a student strike. The event made national news. The college's president resigned, and the new president reinstated the classes. The students had won, and Ronald Reagan had become a celebrity on campus.

Budding Broadcaster

To entertain fraternity brothers, Reagan, with a broomstick for microphone, imitated a radio sportscaster announcing plays on 'the football field.

This joke paid off for him after he graduated in 1932 and was looking for a job. He wanted to broadcast sporting events, and he finally got a tryout at WOC, a small radio station in Davenport, Iowa. For his audition, he had to "broadcast" an imaginary football game and make it sound as real as if he were watching it.

Reagan remembered an exciting game he had played in. He started talking: "Here we are in the fourth quarter with Western State University leading Eureka College six to nothing. . . . Long blue shadows are settling over the field and a chill wind is blowing in through the end of the stadium. . . ."[8] For fifteen minutes he described every play. Then he came to the final play in which he had the responsibility of leading the blocking to open up holes for the ball carrier. In real life, Ronald had missed his block. For this broadcast, he had "Reagan at right guard" make a tremendous block and pave the way for the touchdown.[9]

He got the job. It gave him enough income to buy a car and get an apartment. It was the beginning of a life in which his words would earn him fame and admiration.

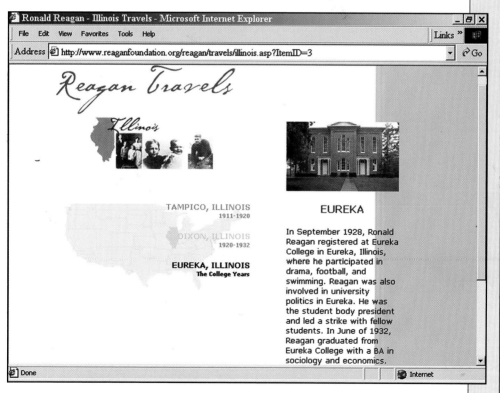

Reagan Travels

Illinois

TAMPICO, ILLINOIS
1911-1920

DIXON, ILLINOIS
1920-1932

EUREKA, ILLINOIS
The College Years

EUREKA

In September 1928, Ronald Reagan registered at Eureka College in Eureka, Illinois, where he participated in drama, football, and swimming. Reagan was also involved in university politics in Eureka. He was the student body president and led a strike with fellow students. In June of 1932, Reagan graduated from Eureka College with a BA in sociology and economics.

▲ *Illinois-born and bred, Reagan did not venture far when he went to college—he attended Eureka College, in Eureka, Illinois. He graduated in 1932 with a degree in sociology and economics.*

Chapter 3 ▶

From Sports to Showbiz to Politics

In 1933, Ronald Reagan transferred from his job in Davenport to one as a sports announcer for radio station WHO in Des Moines, Iowa. Without ever going to the stadium, he specialized in broadcasting baseball games played by the Chicago Cubs. He sat in the booth in a studio with a microphone. In the next room, a telegraph operator received brief telegrams from the actual game and passed them to him. "I then described the play as if I'd been in the press box, even though the slip of paper might say only 'Out 4 to 3'; four was second base and three was first, so it was a grounder to the second baseman who threw the batter out at first."[1] Reagan's job was to flesh out the bare facts and make it seem to the radio listener as if he or she was seeing the game played. Reagan was one of the best practitioners of this art.

▶ No Business Like Show Business

After working only a few years as a radio announcer, Ronald Reagan became interested in Hollywood and the prospect of an acting career. In 1937 he arranged to be assigned by the station to go with the Chicago Cubs to spring training in California.

When he got there, he visited a friend in Hollywood. She called an agent, who called a casting director for Warner Brothers, a leading motion picture company. Reagan was invited to take a screen test, to see how he appeared on film. The screen test went well enough for

Reagan to be signed to a seven-year contract for $200 a week.

Early Films and Marriage

Reagan's early movies were "B" pictures—low-budget movies. The more expensive "A" movies were reserved for the star actors. Reagan had more parts as radio announcers and then played a Secret Service agent named Brass Bancroft in a series of action adventures. The series was so popular that soon Reagan had a fan club of young boys who became members of the "Junior Secret Service Club."

As a sportscaster for radio station WHO in Des Moines, Iowa, Reagan described Chicago Cubs baseball games from the studio as if he were seated within the "friendly confines" of Wrigley Field.

Then Reagan won a part as a football player named George Gipp in the biographical movie *Knute Rockne—All American*. Rockne had been a famous football coach for the University of Notre Dame. The movie was a hit. That same year, 1940, Ronald Reagan married Jane Wyman, an actress who was also under contract to Warner Brothers.

Reagan was also noticed for his role in *King's Row*. He played the town playboy whose legs are amputated after an accident. Reagan's character woke in a hospital bed following surgery, looked down at the flat sheets where his legs were supposed to be, and screamed, "Where's the rest of me?"[2]

The War Effort

In 1941 the United States entered World War II. Having just finished scenes for *Desperate Journey*, in which he and Errol Flynn escaped behind enemy lines, Reagan went into uniform for real. He helped produce propaganda and training films from the Army's own Hollywood studio. He also entertained troops on tour.

Career and Marriage—The Sequel

After the war, Ronald Reagan signed Hollywood's first "million-dollar" contract, which would guarantee him that amount over seven years. Although Reagan commanded a higher salary than his wife, Jane Wyman, she became known as a better actor, whereas Reagan was just a "star." Reagan and Wyman had one daughter, Maureen, born in 1941, and adopted a son, Michael, in 1945.

Reagan wanted to act in Westerns, but the movie studio kept casting him in romantic roles that he was not comfortable with. His "stardom" began to wane as he became involved with the Screen Actors Guild, a union for

Ronald Reagan was a second lieutenant in the Army Reserve when he was called to active duty following the Japanese attack on Pearl Harbor, in December 1941. He served in a noncombat unit of the Army for three years, attaining the rank of captain. He was then transferred to the Army Air Force First Motion Picture Unit, where he narrated training films for bomber pilots.

actors. He served as its president from 1947 to 1952 and 1959 to 1960. In that role, he spent a lot of time negotiating fair contracts for actors.

A Fear of Communism

At the same time, Reagan became convinced that Communists were trying to take over the movie studios and produce Communist propaganda films. The fear that communism would take hold and spread in the United States was fed in 1938 by the formation of the House Un-American Activities Committee. It was formed to root out people disloyal to the American government, but it made accusations against many people without proof or simply because people were associated with certain causes. It was into this climate that federal agents "recruited" Reagan to keep an eye on the activities of those in Hollywood

suspected of being Communists. He filed regular reports on what he observed.

In September 1947, Reagan testified before the House Un-American Activities Committee about the influence of Communists in the movie industry. Not long after that, Jane Wyman divorced him. His political activities apparently added to strains already in the marriage. He told friends that he felt dead inside for several years.[3]

New Marriage, New Career

Eventually, though, he married another actress, Nancy Davis, in March 1952. Their daughter Patti was born later that year, and their son Ronald Prescott was born in 1958.

Reagan's movie career, however, was coming to a close.

In 1954, Reagan was hired as the host of a television program called *General Electric Theater*. Reagan's contract with General Electric called for him to travel about six weeks a year across the

◀ *Ronald Reagan and Nancy Davis, Reagan's second wife, on the set of her film* Donovan's Brain, *in 1953.*

country to visit the company's plants. Often he would make a speech. These speeches more and more became "The Speech," which condemned big government and its taxation system.

▷ Dipping Into Politics

The Speech led Ronald Reagan into politics. Although he had been a staunch Democrat, he decided in 1962 that it was the Republican Party which stood for the principles he admired.

In 1962, his involvement with *General Electric Theater* ended. Some said that Reagan had been fired because his opinions were so strong. That year, Reagan made a speech supporting Richard Nixon for governor of California. Although Nixon lost the election, Reagan made himself even more well known and well liked by voters.

In 1964, Republican Barry Goldwater faced off against Democrat Lyndon Baines Johnson in the presidential race. Just before election day, Reagan made a speech on nation-wide television in support of Goldwater called "A Time For Choosing." It was dramatic, patriotic, and cast the election in terms of good versus evil. Despite Reagan's speech, however, Goldwater lost the election in a flood of votes for Lyndon Johnson.

Reagan had been noticed, however, and after the election, some Michigan conservatives formed a group called "Republicans for Ronald Reagan." He then traveled around California, speaking and listening to ordinary people talk about their problems.

Chapter 4 ▶

A New Role: Citizen-Politician, 1964–1980

By 1966, Ronald Reagan had been nominated to run for governor of California. Pat Brown, the incumbent governor and a Democrat, laughed at having an "actor with makeup" run against him. In one commercial, he told schoolchildren: "I'm running against an actor, and you know who shot Lincoln, don'tcha?"[1]

Reagan used Governor Brown's words to his own advantage. Calling himself a "citizen politician," Reagan directed his campaign at those Californians who were dissatisfied with politics as usual. Californians were unhappy with the state's taxes, and students in the state's universities were rioting. When told that his proposed solutions were simplistic, Reagan said, "There are simple answers, just not easy ones."[2] He won the election easily, getting 58 percent of the vote.

▶ Learning Politics as Governor

As governor, Reagan had to learn politics the hard way. What gave him authority and power was his belief that he could make things better. More experienced politicians resented him, but ordinary citizens loved him.

He soon set the style of governing he would stick with throughout eight years as governor and eight years as president: to set the general principles and goals and hire people he trusted to carry them out. As he discovered later when he was president, that plan did not always work.

▶ Accomplishments as Governor

Reagan had campaigned on a pledge to cut taxes, believing that tax cuts would encourage job development and increase prosperity in the state. However, his duty as governor was to see that the state's bills got paid, and to do that, he had to raise taxes. In this, he faced off against a Democratic majority in the state legislature.

During his years as president of the Screen Actors Guild, Reagan had learned to compromise. As governor, he put those skills to use again. After weeks of hard negotiations and compromises with the legislators, Reagan got

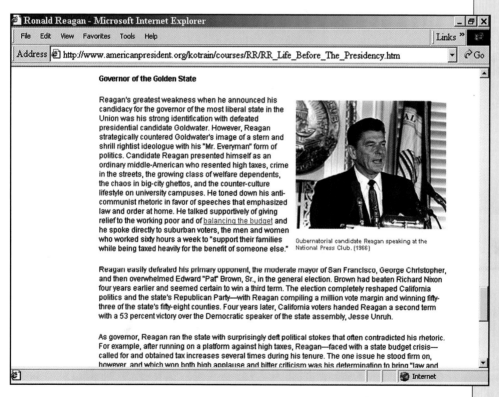

Ronald Reagan - Microsoft Internet Explorer

File Edit View Favorites Tools Help   Links »

Address http://www.americanpresident.org/kotrain/courses/RR/RR_Life_Before_The_Presidency.htm   Go

Governor of the Golden State

Reagan's greatest weakness when he announced his candidacy for the governor of the most liberal state in the Union was his strong identification with defeated presidential candidate Goldwater. However, Reagan strategically countered Goldwater's image of a stern and shrill rightist ideologue with his "Mr. Everyman" form of politics. Candidate Reagan presented himself as an ordinary middle-American who resented high taxes, crime in the streets, the growing class of welfare dependents, the chaos in big-city ghettos, and the counter-culture lifestyle on university campuses. He toned down his anti-communist rhetoric in favor of speeches that emphasized law and order at home. He talked supportively of giving relief to the working poor and of balancing the budget and he spoke directly to suburban voters, the men and women who worked sixty hours a week to "support their families while being taxed heavily for the benefit of someone else."

Gubernatorial candidate Reagan speaking at the National Press Club. (1966)

Reagan easily defeated his primary opponent, the moderate mayor of San Francisco, George Christopher, and then overwhelmed Edward "Pat" Brown, Sr., in the general election. Brown had beaten Richard Nixon four years earlier and seemed certain to win a third term. The election completely reshaped California politics and the state's Republican Party—with Reagan compiling a million vote margin and winning fifty-three of the state's fifty-eight counties. Four years later, California voters handed Reagan a second term with a 53 percent victory over the Democratic speaker of the state assembly, Jesse Unruh.

As governor, Reagan ran the state with surprisingly deft political stokes that often contradicted his rhetoric. For example, after running on a platform against high taxes, Reagan—faced with a state budget crisis—called for and obtained tax increases several times during his tenure. The one issue he stood firm on, however, and which won both high applause and bitter criticism was his determination to bring "law and

Internet

▲ *During his campaign for governor, Candidate Reagan presented himself to the voters of California as one of them—an ordinary, hardworking, middle-class American. His appeal worked—he captured nearly 60 percent of the vote in the California governor's race of 1966.*

the tax increase. He later managed to pass the California Welfare Reform Act in 1971. It reduced the number of people receiving welfare, thus saving the state money.

Even though he was accused of not caring enough about the environment, Reagan made an effort to save California's mighty stands of giant redwood trees. He also stopped a new dam from being built that would have provided more water for Southern California's agriculture, but would have displaced a small tribe of American Indians. Reagan decided that too many treaties with Indians had been broken already, and he would not break another.

▷ Thinking About the Future

Ronald Reagan entered the presidential race in 1968, but the Republican nomination went to Richard Nixon, who also won the presidency. Reagan returned to California and to a second term as governor. Once Nixon took office, however, he sent the Reagans on goodwill missions to foreign countries. Those trips helped prepare Ronald Reagan for the meetings with foreign leaders that he would later have as president himself.

▷ Down at the Ranch

In 1974, near the end of Reagan's second term as governor, Ronald and Nancy Reagan bought a ranch in the Santa Ynez Mountains, north of Santa Barbara, California. There, Ronald Reagan could ride horses, his favorite recreation. He said he could think most clearly when he was on a horse. After serving two terms as governor, from 1967 to 1975, Reagan then waited for the next job to appear. He was sixty-five years old, an age at which many people think of retiring. Reagan, however, thought about running for president. From 1975 to 1979, he gave more than a thousand daily radio broadcasts, calling for a smaller federal government.

Presidential Bids

So in 1976, when he was asked to run for president against other Republicans, including the incumbent, Gerald Ford, he agreed. At the nominating convention in Kansas City, Reagan's votes were slightly fewer than Ford's. But although Ford won the nomination, he lost the election to the Democratic presidential candidate, Jimmy Carter, in November 1976.

Carter's four years in office were marked by a rise in taxes, higher inflation, and increased gasoline prices. By 1980, Ronald Reagan felt that the time had come for him to declare again that he would run for president. And he easily became the Republican nominee at the party's convention in Detroit in July of that year. Reagan chose George H. W. Bush, of Texas, to be his running mate as the vice presidential candidate.

This 1976 photo captures Ronald Reagan where he has always said he is the happiest, at Rancho del Cielo (the "ranch in the sky") nestled in the Santa Ynez Mountains.

▶ The 1980 Presidential Campaign and the Hostage Crisis

During the campaign, Reagan appealed to the frustrated mood of many Americans. "They say the United States has had its day in the sun; that our nation has passed its zenith," he said in one speech. "They expect you to tell your children . . . that the future will be one of sacrifice and few opportunities. My fellow Americans, I utterly reject that view."[3]

A year earlier, on November 4, 1979, more than fifty Americans had been taken hostage and were being held as captives in the U.S. Embassy in Tehran, Iran, after an Islamic revolutionary government had come into power. President Carter had made attempts to free the hostages, but all proved unsuccessful, and one attempted rescue resulted in the deaths of eight American servicemen.

When Reagan and Carter met in a nationally televised debate, Carter accused Reagan of wanting to cut Social Security benefits for the elderly. But Reagan, a master at deflecting criticism, was able to make fun of Carter's comments, saying, "There you go again."[4] The audience loved it. At the debate's end, Reagan scored a decisive victory by asking the viewing public if they thought they were better off than they had been four years earlier. Their answer, judging by the election results on November 4, 1980, was no. It was dinnertime in the Reagans' California home when Carter phoned to concede. Ronald Reagan had become the fortieth president of the United States by winning the electoral vote in forty-four states.

His Best Role: President

In his inaugural speech on January 20, 1981, Reagan referred to government as "not the solution to our problems; government is the problem. . . ."[1] He made the case that not just an elite few but all Americans were responsible for the country's future. After his inauguration, Reagan announced that former President Carter's efforts to free the fifty-two Americans held hostage for 444 days in Iran had at last been successful. The hostage crisis, which had helped Reagan to defeat Carter, was finally over.

▶ A Joke Means "No"

Reagan filled his cabinet with many of the advisors who had served him when he was governor. He wanted them to

◀ A jubilant Ronald and Nancy Reagan during the fortieth president's inaugural parade, January 20, 1981.

debate until they could agree on what he should do. Then he would agree or disagree with their decision.

Reagan's way of saying no in meetings was to interrupt with a funny story or joke. If he remained silent, it usually meant "yes." Sometimes, though, it meant he wanted to think about it some more, preferably on horseback. He used his charm and humor to make journalists, members of Congress, military leaders, and leaders of foreign nations feel as if they were special. He was friendly with everyone, but had few really close friends.

▶ Reaganomics

Reagan soon made good on his campaign promises. He had promised to appoint a woman to the Supreme Court and he did: Sandra Day O'Connor, of the Arizona Court of Appeals. He had also promised to cut taxes, and he succeeded in doing that. The attempt on Reagan's life, on March 30, made him even more popular, and he used that popularity to persuade Congress to pass some of the tax cuts he wanted. They were part of his Program for Economic Recovery. During Reagan's terms in office, his economic program, which was dubbed "Reaganomics," cut inflation and led to the creation of many more jobs. But tax cuts and increased military spending also led to a huge national debt—the largest in the nation's history.

▶ Grounded!

On August 3, 1981, more than 70 percent of nearly 17,000 air-traffic controllers went on strike over negotiations for better pay. Air traffic into and out of many airports was restricted while supervisors and controllers who did not strike tried to keep planes flying. Reagan took a firm stance with the striking controllers by saying that if

Reagan said that he thought best while riding a horse. Here he is pictured riding at Camp David, the presidential retreat in Maryland.

they did not return to work within two days, their jobs would be terminated. He kept that promise: On August 5, he fired more than 11,000 controllers who had not returned to work.

International Problems

Also in August, U.S. Navy planes shot down two Libyan planes that had fired on them. After the Libyan planes were downed, Libyan terrorists sneaked into the United States in a failed attempt to assassinate not only the president but also Vice President George Bush, Secretary of State Alexander Haig, and other administration officials.

In Nicaragua, the Sandinista government in power was trying to spread communism throughout Central America. Reagan approved a plan to recruit and finance guerrilla "freedom fighters" called contras to oppose the Sandinistas. Launched in the first year of Reagan's presidency, the U.S. government's funding of the contras was later found to be connected to an illegal arms-for-hostages deal with Iran.

Ending the Cold War

On September 1, 1983, Korean Air Lines Flight KE007 strayed into Soviet air space, and Soviet planes shot it

down. All on board, including sixty-one Americans, were killed. Reagan called the shooting "an act of barbarism," and he referred to the Soviet Union as an "empire of evil" in his speeches.

Star Wars

The tough rhetoric was preceded by one of Reagan's most startling moves to counter the Soviet nuclear threat. In March 1983, he proposed a strategic nuclear defense system known as the Strategic Defense Initiative. It came to be known as "Star Wars." Reagan tried to convince the country of the need for such a system. In his plan, laser and particle-beam weapons in orbit would destroy Soviet missiles before they could strike. Some experts thought the plan would never work. Others considered it visionary and bold.

Sending in American Troops

In October 1983, in the tiny eastern Caribbean island-nation of Grenada, the country's newly elected president was executed by a Communist force. Concerns mounted for the safety of 600 American students who attended the island's medical school. Other Caribbean states asked the United States to intervene. Reagan sent troops into Grenada that defeated the Communists and freed the students.

At almost the same time, in Lebanon, a suicide bomber drove a truck filled with explosives into a barracks and killed more than two hundred U.S. Marines who had been sent there by Reagan to keep peace. Eventually, the United States withdrew its forces from Lebanon.

Running for a Second Term

Since Dwight Eisenhower's presidency (1952–60), no United States president had been elected to two terms.

Nancy Reagan and some friends thought Ronald Reagan should retire after his first term because they could foresee tough times ahead. But Ronald Reagan felt that only some of his goals had been achieved.

The American public was still high on Reagan, who had become known as the "great communicator" for his skills with the spoken word. The Republicans used that popularity to further Reagan's reelection campaign. They ran a television commercial called "Morning Again in America," which showed heartwarming scenes from American life. As an American flag filled the screen, an announcer said, "It's morning again in America. Today,

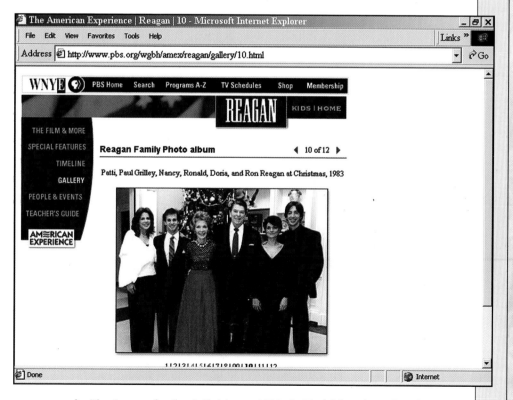

The American Experience | Reagan | 10 - Microsoft Internet Explorer

File   Edit   View   Favorites   Tools   Help   Links »

Address http://www.pbs.org/wgbh/amex/reagan/gallery/10.html   Go

WNYE   PBS Home   Search   Programs A-Z   TV Schedules   Shop   Membership

REAGAN   KIDS | HOME

THE FILM & MORE

SPECIAL FEATURES   **Reagan Family Photo album**   ◀ 10 of 12 ▶

TIMELINE   Patti, Paul Grilley, Nancy, Ronald, Doria, and Ron Reagan at Christmas, 1983

GALLERY

PEOPLE & EVENTS

TEACHER'S GUIDE

AMERICAN
EXPERIENCE

Done   Internet

The Reagan family at Christmas, 1983: Patti and fiancé, Paul Grilley; Nancy and Ronald Reagan; and Doria and Ron Reagan. Reagan's older children, Maureen and Michael, were not present for this photo.

more men and women will go to work than ever before in our country's history. . . . It's morning again in America. And under the leadership of President Reagan, our country is stronger, and prouder, and better. Why would we ever want to return to where we were less than four short years ago?"[2] There was no mention of how Ronald Reagan was going to address the budget deficit, however.

The 1984 Race

In the 1984 presidential race, Reagan was opposed by Walter Mondale, the Democratic candidate. Mondale's position was that the only way to reduce the budget deficit quickly was to raise taxes. Raising taxes was unpopular, but Mondale intended to do it and claimed that Reagan was also planning to raise taxes after the election.

In their first televised debate, Mondale attacked Reagan, who tried to cram too many facts and figures into his presentation to deny what Mondale was saying. Some said that the debate showed that Reagan was too old to be president. However, in the second televised debate, he pulled off another magic moment when a reporter asked whether age was going to be a factor in the campaign. Reagan replied, "I am not going to exploit for political purposes my opponent's youth and inexperience."[3] Even Mondale laughed. He also lost. On November 6, 1984, Ronald Reagan was reelected president, winning forty-nine states and 59 percent of the vote.

Double Trouble—Iran-Contra

But Reagan's second administration was marked by tough times. Iranian militants kidnapped more American hostages and held them in Lebanon. In an attempt to free the hostages without dealing directly with the terrorists,

Reagan approved a controversial program in 1985 of dealing with agents who would act on America's behalf by selling arms to Iran during its war with Iraq. Eventually, however, it turned into selling weapons to terrorists in return for hostages. Although some hostages were freed, even more were taken. Reagan had violated his often-stated promise never to deal with terrorists. To make matters worse, some of the funds from those arms sales were funneled secretly (and illegally) to the Nicaraguan contra rebels who opposed the Sandinista government. The affair became known as the Iran-contra crisis.

Reagan was implicated in the scandal, although no evidence was found linking the president to criminal actions. But other members of the administration were indicted. The special prosecutor appointed by Reagan to investigate the affair and a joint congressional committee reached

Mikhail Gorbachev, left, and Ronald Reagan signing the Intermediate-range Nuclear Forces (INF) Treaty, in the East Room of the White House, December 8, 1987.

the same conclusion, however: that Ronald Reagan's "hands-off" approach to his staff had allowed them to act in a way that they believed the president approved of.

Reagan later apologized to the American people, admitting that trading arms for hostages had been a mistake. In this mistake, all the strengths of Reagan's leadership— his sincerity in opposing communism, his hope to free American hostages, his desire to help achieve a free and peaceful world, his trust in his staff to handle details— combined to appear as weaknesses. The Iran-contra crisis led to talk of impeaching Reagan. But Ronald Reagan was the "Teflon president" to whom guilt just would not stick.[4] Many Americans believed and trusted Ronald Reagan, and his apology made him even more popular among those Americans.

▶ The INF Treaty

Reagan had engaged in meetings in 1985 and 1986 with Mikhail Gorbachev, the Soviet leader, to try to negotiate reductions in nuclear arms. After all, each superpower had nuclear weapons pointed at the other. Between meetings, Reagan sent handwritten notes to try to persuade Gorbachev that both sides could prevent nuclear conflict by drastically cutting back on nuclear weapons. An agreement on arms control was finally reached between the United States and the Soviet Union on December 8, 1987, when Reagan and Gorbachev signed the Intermediate-range Nuclear Forces (INF) Treaty. In that treaty, the two countries agreed to destroy many medium- and short-range missiles and to allow missile site inspections on each other's soil until the end of the twentieth century. As Reagan later wrote, "It was the first time in history that any nations had ever agreed . . . to destroy nuclear missiles."[5]

Reagan's Legacy

After two decades of national sadness—which saw assassinations, the long nightmare of the Vietnam War, and the Iran hostage crisis—Ronald Reagan's presidency helped many Americans feel better about themselves. His administration's policies, however, led to the largest budget deficit in the nation's history, and for the first time in history, the national debt exceeded a trillion dollars.

▶ Charisma

Where Ronald Reagan did succeed was in confirming the power of charisma. His easygoing friendliness appealed to many Americans. To those who made light of his appeal, Reagan said, "Some of my critics . . . have said that I became president because I was an actor who knew how

British prime minister ▶ Margaret Thatcher was one of President Reagan's greatest supporters and a loyal ally during the Reagan years.

to give a good speech. I suppose that's not too far wrong. Because an actor knows two important things—to be honest in what he's doing and to be in touch with the audience. That's not bad advice for a politician either. My actor's instinct simply told me to speak the truth as I saw it and felt it."[1]

▶ What Others Have Said

Margaret Thatcher, a supporter of Ronald Reagan's who was Prime Minister of Great Britain during Reagan's presidency, summed up the fortieth president this way: "When we attempt an overall survey of President Reagan's term of office, covering events both foreign and domestic, one thing stands out. It is that he has achieved the most difficult of all political tasks: changing attitudes and perceptions about what is possible. From the strong fortress of his convictions, he set out to enlarge freedom the world over at a time when freedom was in retreat—and he succeeded."[2]

Mikhail Gorbachev said, years later, "I like Ronald Reagan as a political leader, but on the other hand I was not particularly impressed by his movie roles. His best role was as President."[3]

▶ Into the Sunset

By the summer of 1994, Ronald Reagan knew that something was wrong with his memory. Doctors gave a hopeless diagnosis—he was suffering from Alzheimer's disease, a disease of the central nervous system that would grow progressively worse and that would eventually rob him of his memory. With Nancy's help, he decided to announce his condition. On November 5, 1994, he sat alone and wrote a touching note addressed to the American public.

Ronald Reagan, now a former *president, offers a final salute before boarding a helicopter to leave the Capitol on January 20, 1989.*

My Fellow Americans,

I have recently been told that I am one of the millions of Americans who will be afflicted with Alzheimer's Disease.

Upon learning this news, Nancy and I had to decide whether as private citizens we would keep this a private matter or whether we would make this news known in a public way.

In the past Nancy suffered from breast cancer and I had my cancer surgeries. We found through our open discussions we were able to raise public awareness. We were happy that as a result many more people underwent testing. They were treated in early stages and able to return to normal, healthy lives.

So now, we feel it is important to share it with you. In opening our hearts, we hope this might promote greater awareness of this condition. Perhaps it will encourage a clearer understanding of the individuals and families who are affected by it.

At the moment I feel just fine. I intend to live the remainder of the years God gives me on this earth doing the things I have always done. I will continue to share life's journey with my beloved Nancy and my family. I plan to enjoy the great outdoors and stay in touch with my friends and supporters.

Unfortunately, as Alzheimer's Disease progresses, the family often bears a heavy burden. I only wish there was some way I could spare Nancy from this painful experience. When the time comes I am confident that with your help she will face it with faith and courage.

In closing let me thank you, the American people, for giving me the great honor of allowing me to serve as your President. When the Lord calls me home, whenever that may be, I will leave with the greatest love for this country of ours and eternal optimism for its future.

I now begin the journey that will lead me into the sunset of my life. I know that for America there will always be a bright dawn ahead.

Thank you, my friends. May God always bless you.

Sincerely, Ronald Reagan.[4]

By 1998, when Edmund Morris, a biographer who was well known to Reagan, visited the former president, Morris found that Nancy Reagan's face was the only one that Ronald Reagan recognized. The disease had already taken a terrible toll: Ronald Reagan had forgotten how to read—and had forgotten that he was once president of the United States.[5]

Chapter Notes

Chapter 1. "Honey, I forgot to duck"

1. Edmund Morris, *Dutch* (New York: Random House, 1999), p. 431.

2. Ibid., p. 429.

3. Ibid.

4. Ibid., p. 431.

5. Ibid., pp. 431–432.

6. Ronald Reagan with Richard G. Hubler, *Where's the Rest of Me?* (New York: Cuell, Sloan and Pearce, 1965), p. 6.

7. Morris, p. 432.

Chapter 2. Born "Dutch"

1. Ronald Reagan with Richard G. Hubler, *Where's the Rest of Me?* (New York: Cuell, Sloan and Pearce, 1965), p. 3.

2. Ronald Reagan, *An American Life* (New York: Simon & Schuster, 1990), p. 21.

3. Reagan/Hubler, p. 8.

4. Ibid., pp. 7–8.

5. Reagan, *An American Life*, p. 36.

6. Anne Edwards, *Early Reagan, The Rise to Power* (New York: William Morrow and Company, Inc., 1987), p. 64.

7. Ibid., p. 73.

8. Reagan, *An American Life*, p. 65.

9. Ibid.

Chapter 3. From Sports to Showbiz to Politics

1. Ronald Reagan, *An American Life* (New York: Simon & Schuster, 1990), p. 72.

2. Anne Edwards, *Early Reagan, The Rise to Power* (New York: William Morrow and Company, Inc., 1987), p. 243.

3. Edmund Morris, *Dutch* (New York: Random House, 1999), p. 266.

Chapter 4. A New Role: Citizen-Politician, 1964–1980

1. Lou Cannon, *President Reagan: The Role of a Lifetime* (New York: Simon & Schuster, 1991), p. 45.

2. Ibid., p. 43.

3. Ibid., p. 836.

4. Ibid., p. 141.

Chapter 5. His Best Role: President

1. Ronald Reagan, *An American Life* (New York: Simon & Schuster, 1990), pp. 226–227.

2. Lou Cannon, *President Reagan: The Role of a Lifetime* (New York: Simon & Schuster, 1991), pp. 512–513.

3. Ronald Reagan, *An American Life*, p. 329.

4. Cannon, p. 217.

5. Ronald Reagan, *An American Life*, p. 700.

Chapter 6. Reagan's Legacy

1. Lou Cannon, *President Reagan: The Role of a Lifetime* (New York: Simon & Schuster, 1991), p. 38.

2. Ibid., p. 465.

3. Nick Paumgarten, "Talk of the Town," *The New Yorker*, February 2002, p. 36.

4. Ronald Reagan, handwritten farewell note to the American public, November 5, 1994, full text at the Reagan Library, <http://www.reagan.utexas.edu/resource/handout/Alzheime.htm> (August 29, 2002).

5. Edmund Morris, *Dutch* (New York: Random House, 1999), p. 670.

Further Reading

Adler, Bill, Jr., ed. *The Reagan Wit: The Humor of the American President.* New York: William Morrow & Co., 1998.

Crothers, Lane, and Nancy S. Lind. *Presidents From Reagan Through Clinton, 1981–2001: Debating the Issues in Pro & Con Primary Documents.* Westport, Conn.: Greenwood Publishing Group, 2001.

Johnson, Darv. *The Reagan Years.* Farmington Hills, Mich.: Gale Group, 2000.

Joseph, Paul. *Ronald Reagan.* Minneapolis: ABDO Publishing Company, 1998.

Judson, Karen. *Ronald Reagan.* Berkeley Heights, N.J.: Enslow Publishers, Inc., 1997.

Morris, Edmund. *Dutch: A Memoir of Ronald Reagan.* New York: Random House, 1999.

Reagan, Maureen. *First Father, First Daughter: A Memoir.* New York: Little, Brown & Co., 2001.

Reagan, Ronald. *An American Life: The Autobiography.* New York: Simon & Schuster, 1999.

Robbins, Neal E. *Ronald W. Reagan: Fortieth President of the United States.* Ada, Okla.: Garrett Educational Corporation, 1990.

Wills, Garry. *Reagan's America: Innocents at Home.* New York: Penguin Putnam, 2000.